# LINES AROUND WIMBLEDON

## Vic Mitchell and Keith Smith

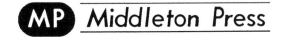

MP Middleton Press

*First published April 1996*

*ISBN 1 873793 75 8*

*© Middleton Press 1996*

*Design - Deborah Goodridge*

*Published by Middleton Press*
          *Easebourne Lane*
          *Midhurst*
          *West Sussex*
          *GU29 9AZ*
          *Tel: 01730 813169*
          *Fax: 01730 812601*

*Printed & bound by Biddles Ltd,*
          *Guildford and Kings Lynn*

# CONTENTS

# INDEX

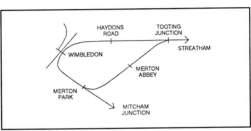

Merton Abbey route to 1929.

Passenger route map for 1955.

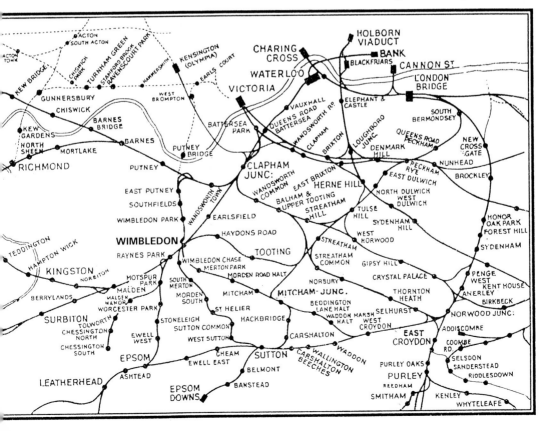

# ACKNOWLEDGEMENTS

We are very grateful for the assistance received from so many of the photographers mentioned in the captions and for the help given by P.G.Barnes, P.Beyer, R.Carpenter, R.M.Casserley, Dr.E.Course, G.Croughton, A.Dasi-Sutton, A.Ll.Lambert, N.Langridge, Mr.D. & Dr.S.Salter, M.Turvey, Miss M. Wheeller, A.Whitehart and C.Wilson. As ever, our wives have been of great support.

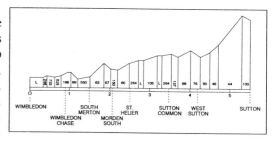

# GEOGRAPHICAL SETTING

The Tooting - Wimbledon and the Tooting-Merton Park routes both crossed the River Wandle, the valley of which was the most industrialised area in Southern England in the eighteenth century, with over 40 water mills producing a diverse range of goods. The railways later served many of these industries. Both lines rose towards Wimbledon, but had no significant gradients.

The Sutton - Wimbledon line starts its course on the Chalk of the dip slope of the North Downs but quickly descends onto London Clay on which the remainder of the line was constructed.

The Putney - Wimbledon route traverses the alluvium and gravels of the Thames Valley and has an undulating course, the middle part of which flanks Wimbledon Park.

All maps are to the scale of 25ins to 1 mile, unless otherwise indicated.

# HISTORICAL BACKGROUND

The three main lines of the area opened as follows. The London & Southampton Railway from London (Nine Elms) to Woking (Common) came into use on 21st May 1838, a station opening at Wimbledon that day. The line became part of the London & South Western Railway in 1839. The London, Brighton & South Coast Railway opened its (West) Croydon to Epsom line through Sutton on 10th May 1847. Finally, the LSWR commenced operating from London to Putney and Richmond on 27th July 1846. All stations in this album opened with their respective sections of line.

The first branch in the district came into use on 22nd October 1855 and was from West Croydon to Wimbledon. It was a LBSCR operation, except in its early years. This company (in conjunction with the LSWR) also extended a branch from Streatham to Wimbledon on 1st October 1868 and provided a link between Merton Park and Tooting on the same day. This gave a pear-shaped route and enabled trains to

run out from, and back to, London without reversal.

Putney Bridge, the line thereon and southwards to Wimbledon was built by the LSWR and opened for District Railway trains on 3rd June 1889. A service of LSWR trains from Waterloo used the route south of East Putney from 1st July of that year.

The Merton Park - Tooting line was closed to passengers on 3rd March 1929. This route, along with the Streatham - Wimbledon section, had been closed to passengers on 1st January 1917, as a wartime economy measure. They were both reopened on 27th August 1923. Closures for freight are detailed in the captions.

The LSWR and LBSCR became part of the Southern Railway in 1923. This company planned some new lines to encourage suburban residential development, but it was to prevent the extension of the District Line that a new line was built between Wimbledon and Sutton. The route between these places was opened southwards to South Merton on 7th July 1929 and on to Sutton on 5th January 1930.

All the lines became part of British Railways upon nationalisation in 1948 and the Putney Bridge - Wimbledon section was transferred to London Underground Ltd on 1st April 1994, when BR was reorganised into small fragments. The other former LSWR line in the area then became part of South West Trains, which was privatised on 4th February 1996.

## Electrification

East Putney - Wimbledon
| | |
|---|---|
| District trains | 27 August 1905 |
| LSWR trains | 25 October 1915 |
| Wimbledon through lines | 30 January 1916 |
| Streatham-Wimbledon | 3 March 1929 |
| West Croydon-Wimbledon | 6 July 1930 |

Sutton-Wimbledon electrified upon opening.

# PASSENGER SERVICES

## Tooting lines

Down train frequencies in the first complete year and in 1890 on the two routes are shown in the table below

| | | 1869 | | 1890 | |
|---|---|---|---|---|---|
| | | Weekdays | Sundays | Weekdays | Sundays |
| LBSCR | via Merton Abbey | 7 | 3 | 12 | 1 |
| | via Haydons Road | 9 | 4 | 2 | 4 |
| LSWR | via Merton Abbey | - | - | 3 | 3 |
| | via Haydons Road | 10 | 4 | 11 | 4 |

Electrification of the route via Haydons Road, after nearly seven years with no trains at all, brought two trains per hour, seven days a week. Apart from reductions in wartime and on Sundays, this frequency has been maintained in most timetables subsequently.

## Sutton to Wimbledon

A daily service of two trains an hour was provided initially, this being continued apart from the restrictions mentioned above. The route was on part of a circular journey from Holborn Viaduct for over 50 years, trains terminating at London Bridge or Victoria.

Thameslink services from North London commenced running round the loop throughout the day in May 1995.

---

February 1890

## East Putney to Wimbledon
### District Line

The first timetable showed two trains per hour on weekdays and Sunday afternoons and by 1904 this frequency was maintained throughout the week.

The electrified service was advertised as about every 10 minutes on weekdays and 15 minutes on Sundays initially, but most commonly comprised 4 or 5 trains per hour in subsequent years.

### LSWR and SR

The table below indicates the frequency of down stopping trains. A few terminated at Wimbledon Park.

| | Weekdays | Sundays |
|---|---|---|
| 1890 | 10 | 8 |
| 1904 | 18 | 15 |
| 1916 | 55 | - |
| 1927 | 12 | - |
| 1938 | 22 | - |
| 1941 | 11 | - |

The service in the mid-1920s and from 11th September 1939 operated in peak hours only. Stopping trains to and from Waterloo were withdrawn on 6th July 1941, as a wartime economy measure, and were never restored. Empty stock and a small number of scheduled passenger trains have used the route subsequently, from time to time, but have not stopped at intermediate stations.

| WIMBLEDON, EAST PUTNEY, and LONDON.—London and South Western. | | | | | | | | | | | | | | | | | | | | | |
|---|---|---|---|---|---|---|---|---|---|---|---|---|---|---|---|---|---|---|---|---|---|
| | mrn | mrn | mrn | aft | aft | aft | aft | aft | aft | | | | | mrn | mrn | aft | aft | aft | aft | aft | aft |
| * Battersea Park. | | | | | | | | | | | | | | | | | | | | | |
| Wimbledon....dep | 8 13 | 9 50 | 1120 | 1 10 | 3 25 | 5 30 | 7 15 | 9 20 | 1035 | .... | ..... | .... | | 8 50 | 1015 | 1150 | 3 20 | 4 45 | 6 10 | 7 40 | 9 10 |
| Wimbledon Park.. | 8 16 | 9 53 | 1123 | 1 13 | 3 28 | 5 33 | 7 18 | 9 23 | 1038 | .... | ..... | .... | | 8 53 | 1018 | 1153 | 3 23 | 4 48 | 6 13 | 7 44 | 9 13 |
| Southfields | 8 19 | 9 56 | 1126 | 1 16 | 3 31 | 5 36 | 7 21 | 9 26 | 1041 | .... | ..... | .... | | 8 56 | 1021 | 1156 | 3 26 | 4 51 | 6 16 | 7 47 | 9 16 |
| East Putney ..... | 8 22 | 9 59 | 1129 | 1 19 | 3 34 | 5 39 | 7 24 | 9 29 | 1044 | .... | ..... | .... | | 8 59 | 1024 | 1159 | 3 29 | 4 54 | 6 19 | 7 50 | 9 19 |
| Wandsworth | 8 25 | 10 2 | 1132 | 1 22 | 3 38 | 5 42 | 7 27 | 9 32 | 1047 | .... | ..... | .... | | 9 2 | 1027 | 12 2 | 3 32 | 4 57 | 6 22 | 7 53 | 9 22 |
| Clapham Junction. | 8 28 | 10 5 | 1134 | 1 24 | 3 40 | 5 45 | 7 30 | 9 34 | 1050 | .... | ..... | .... | | 9 5 | 1030 | 12 5 | 3 35 | 5 0 | 6 25 | 7 56 | 9 25 |
| Queen's Road*.... | 8 31 | 10 8 | 1137 | 1 27 | 3 43 | 5 48 | 7 33 | 9 37 | 1053 | .... | ..... | .... | | 9 8 | 1033 | 12 8 | 3 38 | 5 3 | 6 28 | 8 0 | 9 28 |
| Vauxhall | 8 34 | 1011 | 1140 | 1 29 | 3 46 | 5 51 | 7 36 | 9 40 | 1056 | .... | ..... | .... | | 9 11 | 1036 | 1211 | 3 41 | 5 6 | 6 31 | 8 3 | 9 31 |
| Waterloo ......arr | 8 40 | 1017 | 1146 | 1 35 | 3 52 | 5 58 | 7 42 | 9 46 | 11 2 | .... | ..... | .... | | 9 17 | 1042 | 1218 | 3 47 | 5 12 | 6 37 | 8 10 | 9 38 |

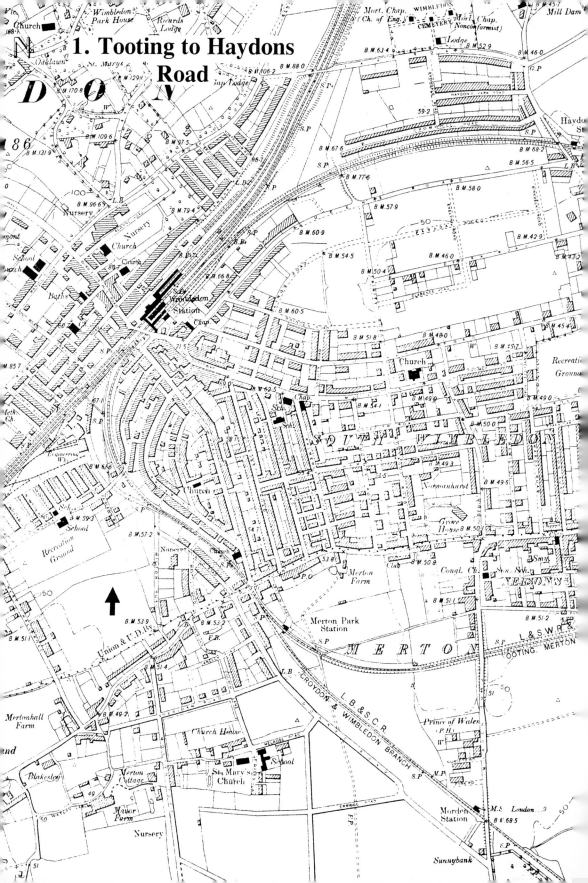

# 1. Tooting to Haydons Road

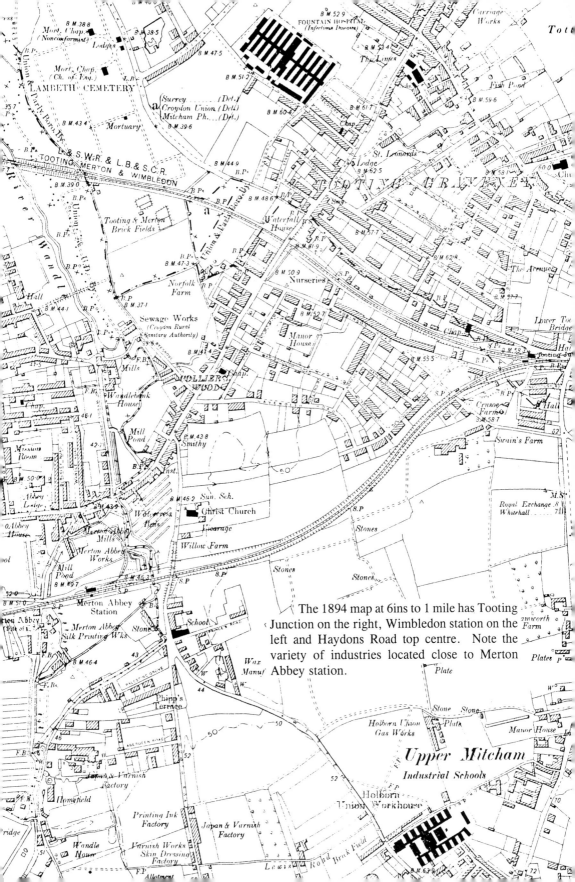

The 1894 map at 6ins to 1 mile has Tooting Junction on the right, Wimbledon station on the left and Haydons Road top centre. Note the variety of industries located close to Merton Abbey station.

# TOOTING

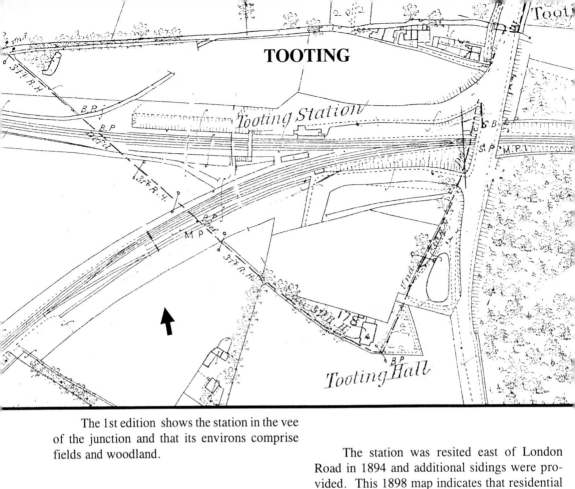

The 1st edition shows the station in the vee of the junction and that its environs comprise fields and woodland.

The station was resited east of London Road in 1894 and additional sidings were provided. This 1898 map indicates that residential development was starting.

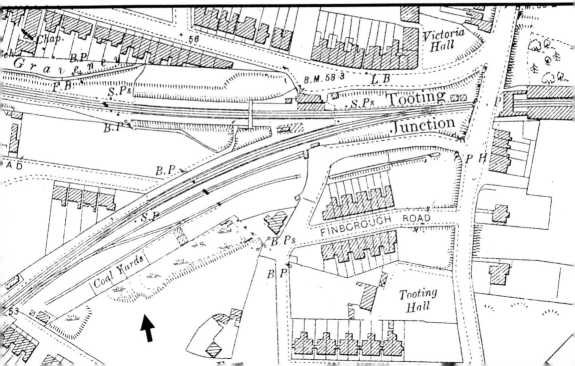

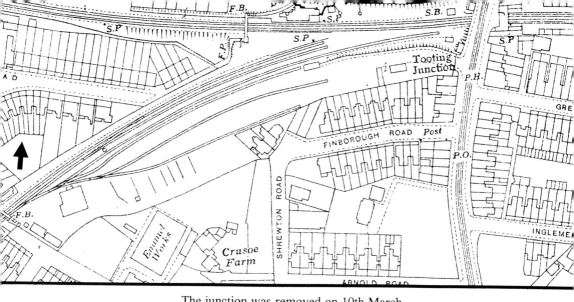

The junction was removed on 10th March 1934, this survey being made later that year. Most building plots were occupied by that time and a further coal siding had been added.

1. The 1894 station entrance is on the right of this postcard view. Railway revenue was severely reduced following the opening of the electric tramway in June 1907. This is fully illustrated in the Middleton Press album *Kingston and Wimbledon Tramways*. (Lens of Sutton)

2. With the 1894 station in the background, ex-SECR class H 0-4-4T no. A329 heads towards Merton Abbey on its way to Wimbledon in the late 1920s. The original platforms are in the foreground. (Lens of Sutton)

3. The original building is seen in this and the next picture after the junction had been removed in 1934. The footbridge was retained, as it carried a public footpath. (D.Cullum coll.)

4. A Wimbledon-bound 4SUB passes the signal box and the site of the junction on 2nd June 1959. In its final years, the box was open only for the morning peak traffic. The 1868 station building was retained for residential purposes. The signal box closed on 27th November 1966. (R.C.Riley)

5. The goods yard remained open until 5th August 1968, trains reaching it via Merton Park. This 1955 view has the roof of the passenger station in the distance, on the right. (N.L.Browne)

6. The goods shed is at the far end of the row of vans in the previous picture. Adjacent to it is the goods crane, which was of 30 cwt capacity. Leaning against the end of the shed is a "Jim Crow", used for bending rails. (J.J.Smith)

7. Standing on the siding seen in the foreground of the previous picture is class U 2-6-0 no. 31639 with the Maunsell Commemorative Rail Tour on 3rd January 1965. The train had started at Waterloo and continued via Virginia Water, Reading South, Redhill, Tonbridge, Oxted and the Mid-Kent Line to London Bridge. (G.Gundry coll.)

8. The new building opened on 12th August 1894 and the word "Junction" was dropped from the station name on 1st March 1938, nine years after it had ceased to function as such. This is the prospective passenger's view in the 1970s. (C.Hall)

9. The building and canopies were intact when class 455 unit no. 5808 was recorded on 4th June 1991, when working the 09.30 Victoria to London Bridge service. The pole on the left carries a CCTV camera. (J.Scrace)

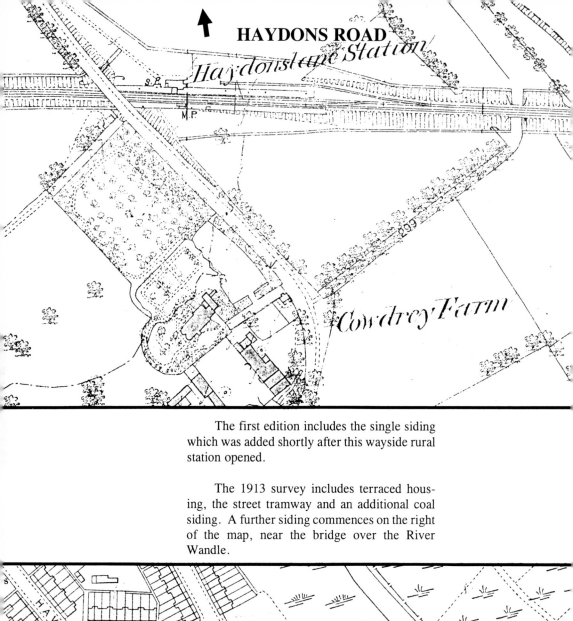

# HAYDONS ROAD

*Haydonslane Station*

*Cowdrey Farm*

The first edition includes the single siding which was added shortly after this wayside rural station opened.

The 1913 survey includes terraced housing, the street tramway and an additional coal siding. A further siding commences on the right of the map, near the bridge over the River Wandle.

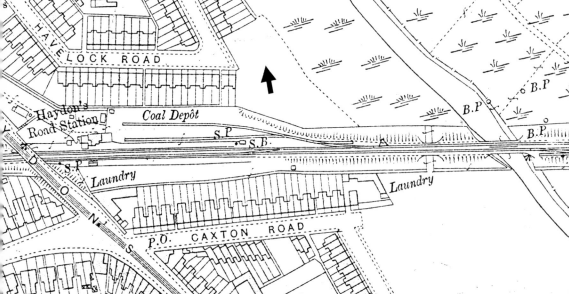

HAVELOCK ROAD

Haydon's Road Station

Coal Depôt

S.P.

S.B.

B.P.

B.P.

B.P.

Laundry

Laundry

P.O. CAXTON ROAD

10. The main buildings were on the up platform. Traffic was very light for many years;
for example the revenue in 1928 was under £300
but in 1933 it was over £5000. (Lens of Sutton)

The siding on the right of the previous map
was about 250 yards long and first served a
brickworks. It was later used by the Wandle
Valley Joint Sewerage Board and also by the
contractors for the Northern Line extension for
a short period.

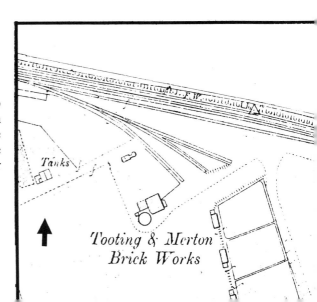

Tanks

Tooting & Merton
Brick Works

11.  The foot crossing was removed and steps to the road were provided from each platform prior to electrification. This station and Tooting Junction were staffed by the LSWR; Merton Park and Merton Abbey had LBSCR men prior to 1923.  (Lens of Sutton)

12.  Class R1 0-4-4T no. A706 (ex-SECR) approaches with a London Bridge to Wimbledon train on 12th May 1927.  The chimney of the brickworks is in the distance.  (H.C.Casserley)

13. A special train of Pullman cars from Victoria to Southampton Docks passed through on 2nd May 1953, hauled by no. 34065 *Hurricane*. Both the station and the locomotive had electric lighting. The signal box (left) closed on 29th March 1967, the goods yard having ceased to handle traffic on 5th December 1966. (D.Cullum)

14. The SR provided new buildings, canopies and signal box. There was once a substantial traffic to a nearby football ground and greyhound race track. In 1933, 93552 tickets were issued, but 48657 more were collected owing to incoming passengers having return tickets. (F.Hornby)

15. No. 319038 passes the new building and the old shelter on 4th June 1991, as it works the 10.00 Victoria to London Bridge circular service via Sutton. The name was officially "Hayden's Lane" until 1st October 1889, contrary to the Ordnance Survey record. (J.Scrace)

16. Having some architectural style, the new up side office was an improvement on its predecessor. The environs were also improved to attract passengers who would soon be able to travel direct to the City again, and also Kings Cross. (J.Scrace)

# 2. Merton Abbey to Merton Park

## MERTON ABBEY

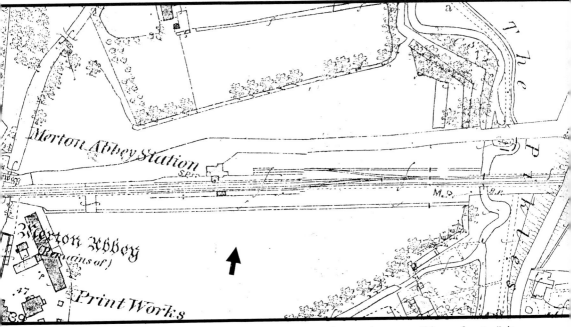

The first edition indicates that the station and its single siding were surrounded by fields and embraced by rivers - the Wandle on the left and The Pickles on the right. "Remains" of the abbey are shown; the next edition refers to "site of". Records state that it was a priory, however, and was in use from 1136 until the dissolution. King Henry VI was crowned there.

17. Ex-LSWR 0-4-4T no. E251 of class M7 waits for the down starting signal to clear before propelling the two former LSWR coaches to Wimbledon. This (and the next picture) was taken on 23rd August 1927. Track maintenance on the 1868 lines was undertaken in alternate five-year periods by the LSWR and LBSCR. (H.C.Casserley)

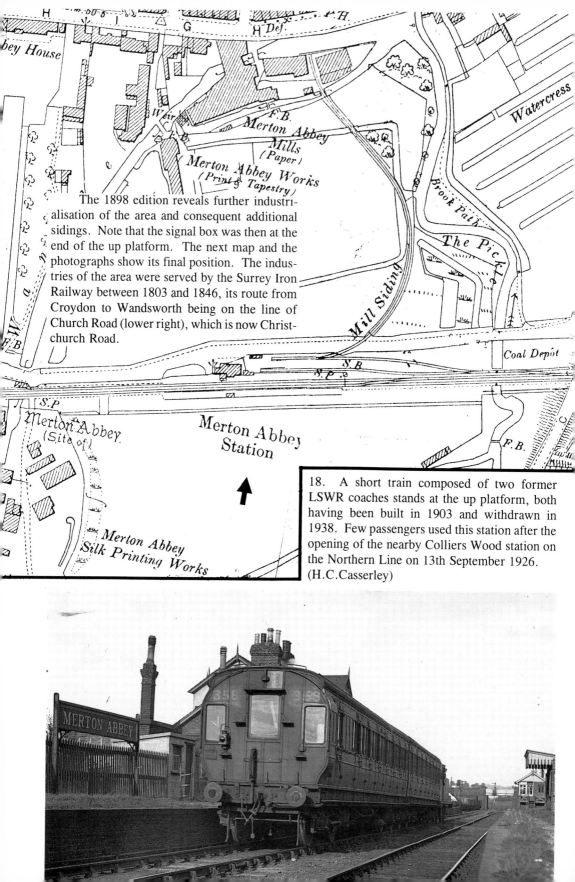

The 1898 edition reveals further industrialisation of the area and consequent additional sidings. Note that the signal box was then at the end of the up platform. The next map and the photographs show its final position. The industries of the area were served by the Surrey Iron Railway between 1803 and 1846, its route from Croydon to Wandsworth being on the line of Church Road (lower right), which is now Christchurch Road.

18. A short train composed of two former LSWR coaches stands at the up platform, both having been built in 1903 and withdrawn in 1938. Few passengers used this station after the opening of the nearby Colliers Wood station on the Northern Line on 13th September 1926. (H.C.Casserley)

19. After the cessation of passenger services in 1929, the signals were removed but the box remained standing. The station building was used as a goods office and as a dwelling. The Merton Relief Road now occupies most of the route. (Lens of Sutton)

20. This example of the SECR C class was not uncommon power on goods services until diesels began to appear in 1959. The LBSCR C2X class 0-6-0s were seen more regularly. The leading wagon is for cattle, surprising in this industrial area. (Lens of Sutton)

21. A westward view from Christchurch Road bridge includes the gantry crane and the down platform, denuded of shelter and signal box. The girders in the foreground carry the tracks over The Pickle. In 1959, freight trains departed at 9.0am and 7.40pm Mondays to Fridays and at 6.15pm on Saturdays. (Lens of Sutton)

22. The SCTS "South Londoner" railtour made an unusual sight at the up platform on 20th April 1958. The push-pull set was worked by class H 0-4-4T no. 31521, a former SECR engine. (J.H.Aston)

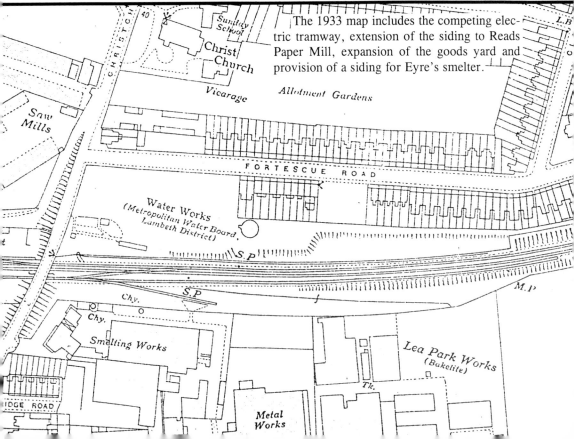

The 1933 map includes the competing electric tramway, extension of the siding to Reads Paper Mill, expansion of the goods yard and provision of a siding for Eyre's smelter.

23. The up line to Merton Park was taken out of use on 3rd November 1935 and the buffer stop on the left was installed. This view is from the level crossing close to the bridge over the River Wandle. Traffic ceased to Merton Abbey on 1st May 1972. The line falls at 1 in 240 to the bridge and rises at 1 in 313 beyond it. (J.J.Smith)

Between Merton Abbey and Merton Park was the siding for Lines Bros, toy manufacturers noted for their range of Minic road vehicle models. The bridge carries Morden Road and the map is from 1933.

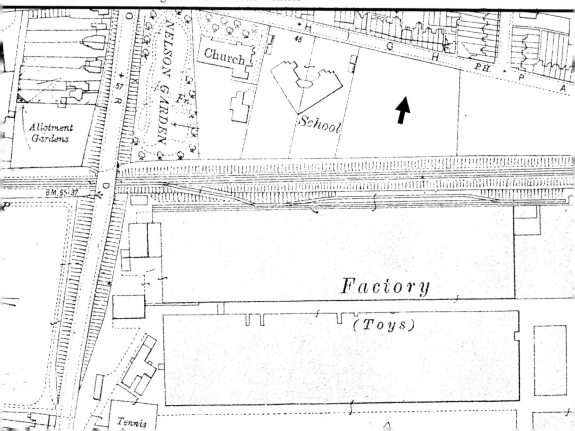

# MERTON PARK

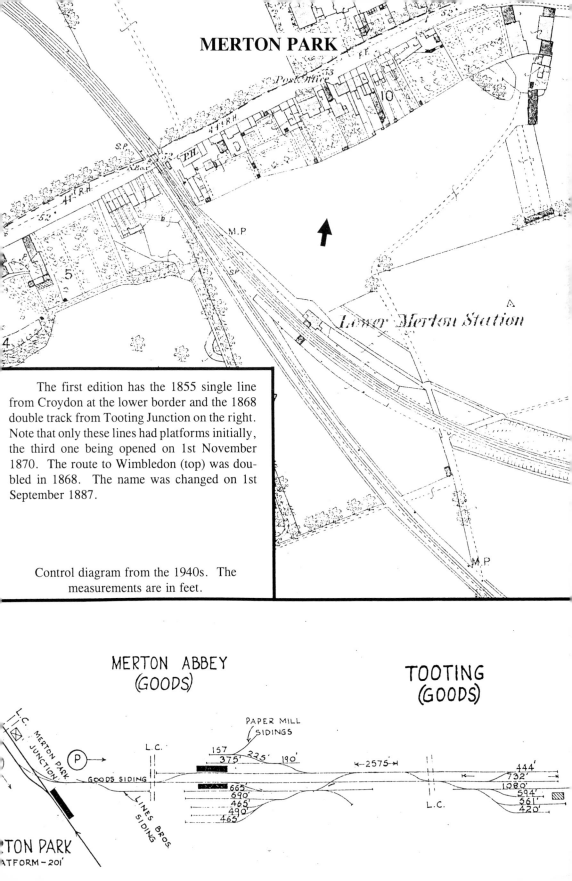

*Post Office*

M.P

Lower Merton Station

M.P

The first edition has the 1855 single line from Croydon at the lower border and the 1868 double track from Tooting Junction on the right. Note that only these lines had platforms initially, the third one being opened on 1st November 1870. The route to Wimbledon (top) was doubled in 1868. The name was changed on 1st September 1887.

Control diagram from the 1940s. The measurements are in feet.

MERTON ABBEY
(GOODS)

TOOTING
(GOODS)

PAPER MILL
SIDINGS

L.C.
MERTON PARK JUNCTION

P

L.C.          157   375'  225'  190'          ←―2575―→                                    444'
                                                                                           732'
GOODS SIDING                              665'                                             1080'
                                          690'                          L.C.              594'
LINES BROS. SIDING                        465'                                            561'
                                          490'                                            420'
                                          465'

:TON PARK
\TFORM – 201'

24.   LSWR class T1 0-4-4T no. 61 waits to depart with a train for Ludgate Hill via Tulse Hill and Herne Hill on 9th August 1906.  This locomotive was in use from 1888 until 1932. (Lens of Sutton)

25.  The building received a number of additions over the years but was basically similar to the one at Merton Abbey.  The residents of the fine villas in Station Road had a good choice of destinations from the nearby station. (Lens of Sutton)

26. The last train from Ludgate Hill was recorded on 2nd March 1929. This former LSWR service was being worked by ex-SECR class H 0-4-4T no. A 164 hauling SECR-built coaches. The booking office contained the single line staff instrument for the line to Mitcham, released from the signal box. (H.C.Casserley)

27. Taken on the same day, this picture features class M7 no. 243 working one of the last up trains, while one resident prefers to turn his back on it. The reopening of these platforms had lasted less than six years. (H.C.Casserley)

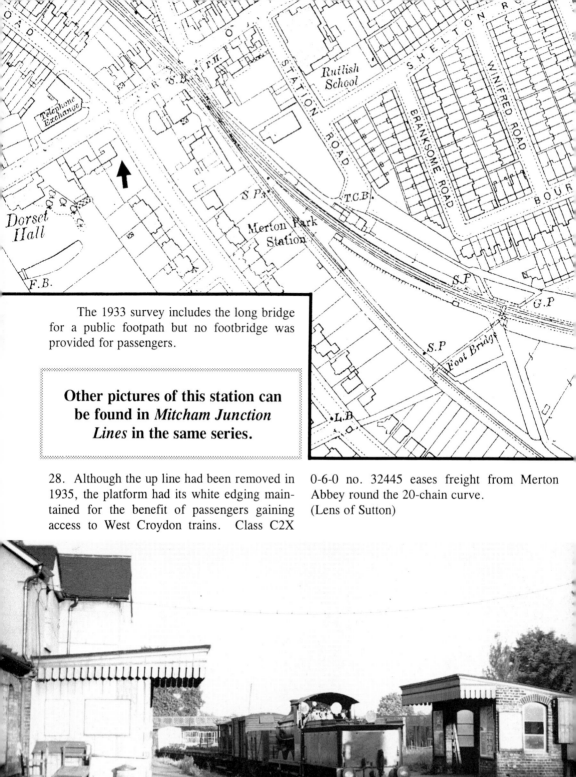

The 1933 survey includes the long bridge for a public footpath but no footbridge was provided for passengers.

**Other pictures of this station can be found in *Mitcham Junction Lines* in the same series.**

28.  Although the up line had been removed in 1935, the platform had its white edging maintained for the benefit of passengers gaining access to West Croydon trains.   Class C2X 0-6-0 no. 32445 eases freight from Merton Abbey round the 20-chain curve.
(Lens of Sutton)

29.  As at Merton Abbey, a wind break was provided at the west end of the canopy. The up trackbed was becoming a nature reserve when photographed on 1st June 1962. Most passengers used the foot crossing shown in the next picture, although some used the more direct staff crossing. (J.Scrace)

30.  Unit no. 5757 is working from West Croydon to Wimbledon on 9th August 1972 and is approaching the Kingston Road level crossing and Merton Park signal box. The latter closed on 23rd May 1982. The goods line from Merton Abbey joins at the point where the double track to Wimbledon commences. (T.Wright)

31. Looking from an approaching train in 1987, it is evident that the foot crossing was cleared away following removal of the goods line. A bank was made between the two disused platforms to carry a path, the end of which is near the seat. (A.C.Mott)

32. There is one other level crossing to pass over before trains reach Wimbledon. This is it, at Dundonald Road. It is on a 14-chain curve and was automated in 1982. The class 415 LSWR 4-4-2Ts became well known on the Lyme Regis branch but in earlier years there was a large fleet working suburban services. Four were fitted for push-pull working. This is no. 058, which is propelling a train from Wimbledon to Ludgate Hill on 21st June 1924. It is carrying a red rear lamp. (H.C.Casserley)

# 3. Sutton to Wimbledon West Yard

## SUTTON

33. This important station has had a complex evolution which is outlined in our *West Croydon to Epsom* album. The platforms serving that route are seen in April 1928 with ex-LBSCR class D1 0-4-2T no. B282 and a railmotor coach. The station facade is in the right background. Overhead electrification was in use on these tracks from 1925 until 1929. (H.F.Wheeller)

34. The station building was replaced by this structure in 1928-29, in readiness for the opening of the new line from Wimbledon on 5th January 1930. The four platforms remained little altered. (Lens of Sutton)

35. Conductor rails arrived in 1928 and were extended to the South Coast ten years later allowing 4 COR units of this type to call. Here is the 10.23am from Portsmouth Harbour on 24th May 1939. Such twelve-coach trains necessitated platform lengthening. The second vehicle is in lighter green than the others and is a buffet car. (J.R.W.Kirkby)

The 1913 map has the Epsom line on the left. The junction for the Wimbledon line was laid later in this area. The Epsom Downs branch is at the lower border, the Mitcham Junction route is right (upper) and the West Croydon pair right (lower). The bottom line is the headshunt for the goods yard, which closed on 7th October 1968.

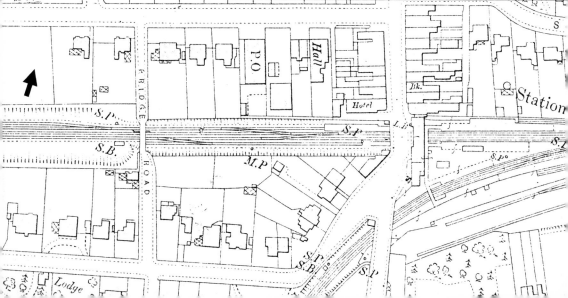

36. A 4SUB departing towards West Croydon is seen from the up Epsom Downs platform in January 1971. Sutton Junction Box (centre) and the semaphore signals remained in use until 3rd October 1982. (R.E.Ruffell)

Other Middleton Press albums to include this station are *Steaming through Surrey*, *Mitcham Junction Lines* and *West Croydon to Epsom*.

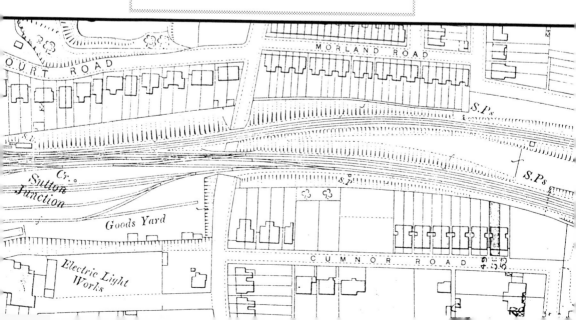

# SUTTON WEST JUNCTION

37. The box on the left was at the commencement of quadruple track, all dating from 1899. The box was originally named "Sutton Main Line". The widening of the chalk cutting to provide space for a junction for the Wimbledon line in 1928 required the provision of a substantial retaining wall and a shortening of the quadruple track. (Lens of Sutton)

38. A class 415 unit drops down the 1 in 44 gradient and will soon face a 13-chain curve. It is these features that give the line the name "The Wall of Death" in the railway world. Also seen in this 1984 photograph are the weight-reducing holes in the bridge. Sutton West Box closed on 17th July 1955. (F.Hornby)

39. 4SUB no. 4319 approaches the junction in 1950 while working a Holborn Viaduct - West Croydon service. One front window was openable to allow stencil changing. It served an additional purpose in hot weather. These 1925 units were formed of three cars until the late 1940s. (F.Hornby)

WEST SUTTON

Tennis Court

West Sutton Station

L.B.

S.B.

Running

Tennis Courts

Tennis Grounds

Bowling Green

Tennis Courts

NORMAN ROAD

ST JAMES' AVENUE

ST JAMES' ROAD

F.F.

The 1933 survey indicates that a large amount of land was retained for recreational purposes. The railway revenue would have been better had more houses been built.

40. The fireplace on the left of this October 1928 view is evidence that a number of homes had to be sacrificed, despite the railway having been planned back in 1910. (Lens of Sutton)

41. The stark outline of the new station was in contrast with one of the few old board-clad houses of the district. The semi-detached design was the predominant new style in the area.

Sutton United Football Club's ground was adjacent to the station and the railway gained revenue as a result. (Lens of Sutton)

42. As at the new junction, substantial retaining walls were required to minimise disruption to private property. On the left is the side of the building seen in the previous picture. It was demolished in 1990. The distant signal is for the junction. The house on the right was occupied by the station master, who was responsible for the entire line. (Lens of Sutton)

43. Other important functions of the staff here included signalling to the guard of an up train that it was ready to depart, as the curvature limited his vision. (F.Hornby coll.)

44. Class N 2-6-0 no. 31412 worked this football special from High Wycombe on its journey south from Kensington Olympia on 3rd February 1962. It continued with the empty coaches to Stewarts Lane via Tooting and returned with them via Sutton, to avoid having to climb the 1 in 44 gradient seen in pictures 38 and 39. (Lens of Sutton)

45. Looking from almost the same viewpoint on 26th May 1988, we see the 16.31 Thameslink service from St. Albans and that the buildings have been boarded up following destaffing. A few Monday - Friday afternoon trains commenced north of the Thames from that month until regular services started seven years later. (F.Hornby)

46. Sir Robert McAlpine & Sons were the main contractors; their work started in July 1928. Over 120,000 cu. yds. of material had to be moved and for this purpose a 3ft 6ins gauge railway was laid. This is their no. 12, which was built by Hudswell Clark in 1913. (H.F.Wheeller)

47. No. 64 was an 0-6-0T by the same manufacturer. It was given the works no. 1573 when built in 1925. Great difficulty was experienced with a thin strata of unstable blue clay in this vicinity. (H.F.Wheeller)

48. Local residents had dust or mud to complain about, depending on the weather, but always had to endure noise and disruption. Excavators were then still known as "steam navvies". (R.Shepherd)

The 1933 map shows mostly semi-detached dwellings with a few larger houses.

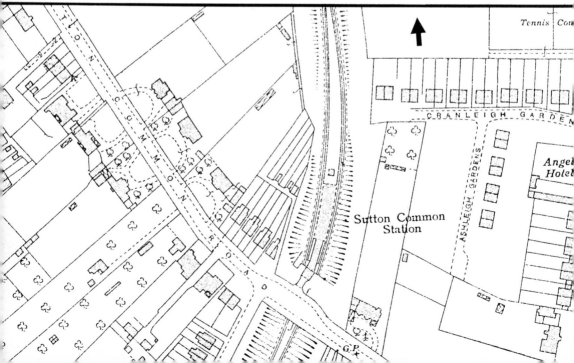

49. This southward view is at the commencement of one of the many cuttings on the route. The curvature here is fairly severe at 22 chains; worse is to follow for down trains. (Lens of Sutton)

50. Approaching Sutton Common on 5th June 1966 is no. 34089 *602 Squadron* with the Southern Counties Touring Society's "Surrey Rambler". It had run from Victoria via Redhill, Guildford, Chertsey, Hounslow, Crystal Palace, Norwood Junction and Epsom Downs and would continue via Tooting and Longhedge to Victoria. (S.C.Nash)

51. Until June 1963, two night trains called at this island platform - the 1.35am Herne Hill to Sutton and the 3.40am Sutton to Victoria. Toilet facilities were available at all stations on the route. (Lens of Sutton)

# ST. HELIER

The London County Council built 10000 small houses in this district in order to reduce the number of inner city slums. Keen to have a station provided here, the LCC offered the SR 12 acres of land free of charge. It was the only one on the route to have a goods yard, but the proposed goods shed was never built. This 1933 edition includes both crossovers; one was still in place in 1995.

52. Although on the fringe of the St. Helier Estate, there were many shops nearby and the station was a good traffic centre, despite the fact that most trains terminated in the City. (Lens of Sutton)

53. The RCTS "South London" railtour on 30th September 1950 was hauled by class C 0-6-0 no. 31722. It was piloted by class E6 0-6-2T no. 32418 from St. Helier to West Croydon. Part of the goods yard is visible; this closed on 6th May 1963. The signal box was the only one on the new line and closed on 23rd May 1982. (J.J.Smith)

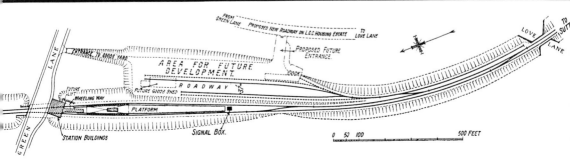

54. A 1964 photograph records SR architecture at its worst. The Chessington South branch was the next major development when the island platform concept was abandoned and some attempts at styling were made. (J.N.Faulkner)

55. After collecting the empty tanks from the Express Dairy siding at Morden, the Clapham Junction milk train had to continue to St. Helier to run round using the two crossovers south of the station. BR class 4 4-6-0 no. 75078 (carrying the "via East Putney" headcode) has just completed this manoeuvre on 24th October 1964 and its train is crossing to the up line towards Wimbledon. Meanwhile the signalman has allowed the 12.37pm from Holborn Viaduct into the down platform. (J.N.Faulkner)

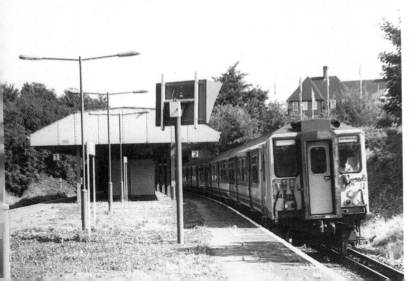

56. Class 455 no. 5842 is working a London Bridge to Victoria service on 20th August 1992, displaying an incorrect destination. Some trains have terminated here, for example the 10.14am from Holborn Viaduct on Saturdays in 1930 and the 12.19am train from Holborn Viaduct in 1963. (F.Hornby)

# MORDEN SOUTH

57. There were 33 bridges on the five miles of new route, most being of concrete construction. This exception was to span the A24. It required 280 tons of steel, the main girders being 135ft long. (Lens of Sutton)

58. Access to the platform is via a subway from London Road (left). The Express Dairy (right) had a siding from 27th March 1954 and its own locomotive, visible below the chimney. There was a two-lever ground frame, released by St. Helier box. (Lens of Sutton)

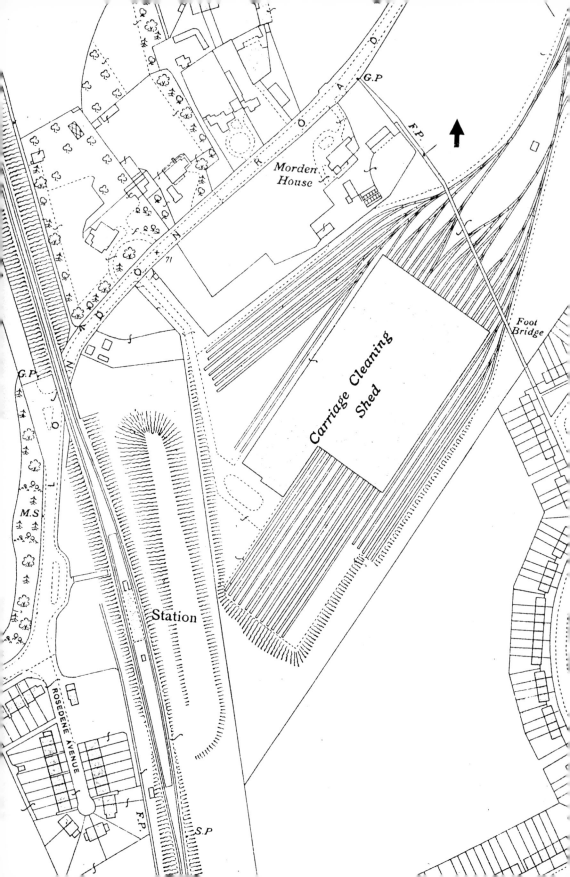

G.P

A

O

R

Morden
House

N

71

D

N

O

J

M.S

Station

ROSEDENE AVENUE

F.P

S.P

G.P

F.P

Carriage Cleaning
Shed

Foot
Bridge

59. Milk tank wagons and the dairy's Hunslet diesel shunter are evident as are the company's three sidings. Loaded tankers were conveyed direct but empty ones had to return via St. Helier, as seen in picture no. 55. Traffic declined and ceased in the early 1970s.
(Lens of Sutton)

The 1933 map has Morden South station on the left and a spoil heap east of it. This was to become the site of the dairy. On the right (on a lower level) are the Northern Line carriage sidings, completed in 1929. District Line trains were to have been based here in the original plan.

60. A down train arrives on 20th February 1995 in the form of class 455 no. 5838 working the 14.03 from London Bridge to Victoria. In the background is the top of the bridge seen in picture no. 57. Ticket sales increased here five-fold in the first five years, season tickets increasing by a factor of ten. (M.J.Stretton)

61. Martin Way bridge had risen in the background and the temporary way had been replaced by a single track permanent way when the new platform edges were recorded on 26th March 1929. (H.C.Casserley)

The three roads that intersected at this point had to be raised by up to 24 ft, the embankments requiring 80000cu. yds. of material. The surrounding land was still to be developed when this survey was made in 1933.

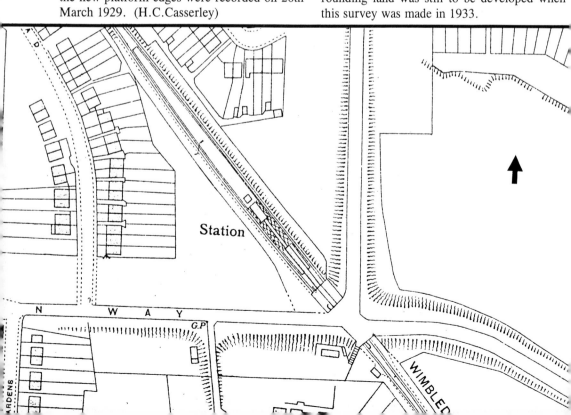

62. A down train stands at the up platform soon after the opening, the "H" surmounted by a dot indicating that it is working from Victoria to London Bridge. The bank on the left is for Mostyn Road and that on the right is for Martin Way, then Green Lane. (H.F.Wheeller)

63. Class 415 (4EPB) no. 5446 runs south on 1st April 1984. These units served South London well from their introduction in 1957 until the final journey on 15th April 1995. Semis dominate the scene. Intermediate block colour light signals were provided here. The small booking office was on the platform. (F.Hornby)

64.  The opportunity to purchase the last traditional Edmondson card ticket to be issued on the Southern Region was given to Keith Smith, as coauthor of a large number of books on that system.  The date was 28th July 1988.  Thomas Edmondson had issued the first in 1837, on the Newcastle & Carlisle Railway.  (British Rail)

# WIMBLEDON CHASE

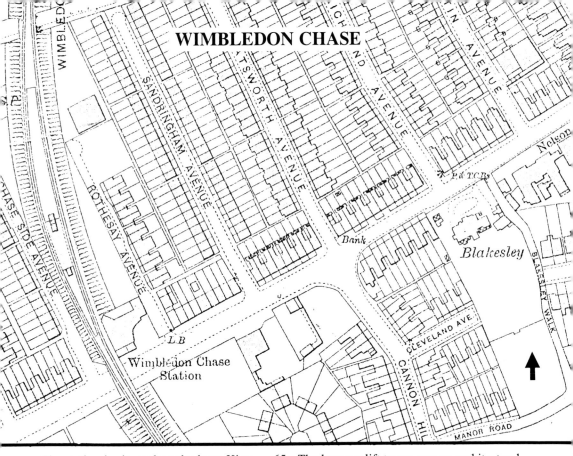

The station is situated on the busy Kingston Road and the area was well populated when this map was drawn in 1933. Rothesay Avenue and Chase Side Avenue were built after the railway.

65. The luggage lift tower was an architectural feature but, like the new stations on the Chessington branch, it never contained any mechanism. The shops await occupation. (British Rail)

66. The train seen in picture no. 50 is approaching the up platform and is running on the 1½ miles of embankment that was built by SR engineers ahead of the main contract. They started in October 1927 and conveyed 120,000 cu. yds. of fill from a variety of sites on the system. (Lens of Sutton)

67. A down train rounds the 17-chain curve on 20th August 1992. Running sands in this vicinity necessitated piling to a depth of up to 35ft under the station and bridge abutments. (F.Hornby)

0487

BRITISH RAILWAYS (S)
Perambulator or Child's Mail
Cart accompanying Passenger
at Owner's risk
FROM ANY STATION
NOT EXCEEDING
5 MILES DISTANT to
WIMBLEDON CHASE
Rate 8d. D
FOR CONDITIONS
SEE BACK
- - - - - - - - - - - - - -
BRITISH RAILWAYS (S)
Perambulator or Child's Mail
Cart accompanying Passenger
at Owner's risk
Wimbledon Chase to
ANY STATION NOT
EXCEEDING
5 MILES DISTANT
Rate 8d. D
FOR CONDITIONS
SEE BACK
0487

# WIMBLEDON WEST YARD

68. During the final stages of the completion of the line to Sutton, the SR used ex-SECR P class no. A556. It is seen taking water from a hydrant on 26th March 1929. The locomotive was used by BR until 1960 and is now on the Kent & East Sussex Railway. Nos A555 and A558 were also used on this work. (H.C.Casserley)

69. The Morden South to Clapham Junction empty milk tank train is behind C class no. 31495 on 12th March 1960 as it waits to cross to the East Putney line, using the crossover shown in the next picture. The white building was a seaplane hanger at Newhaven during World War I and was bought by the LBSCR subsequently. It was re-erected here in 1935 to house the workshops of the Signal & Telegraph Dept. (J.N.Faulkner)

The quadruple tracks from Woking are on the left and below them is "C" Box and the curved lines from Wimbledon Chase. On the right is "B" Box and the road bridge west of the station. The curve lower right on this 1933 map is for Merton Park trains. Various railway departments have used the buildings marked "Engineering Works". Public traffic ceased at the goods yard on 5th January 1970. Continue to picture no. 110 for Wimbledon station.

70. Class 4 4-6-0 no. 75069 stands in "Volunteer" siding on 14th May 1964. The platform received this name when it was used by soldiers on manoeuvres on Wimbledon Common prior to WWI. It was raised in 1926 for use as a milk dock. As part of the Waterloo Area Resignalling Scheme, an industrial-style building was erected beyond the left border of this picture and the first panel therein came into use on 5th February 1984. "B" Box (left of centre) was in use until 23rd May 1982. (J.Scrace)

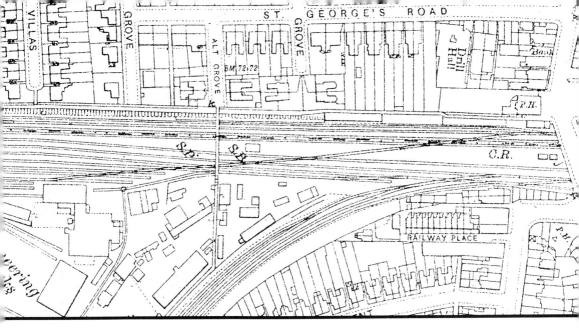

71. Two dirty 2SAP units pass Wimbledon "C" Box on 26th September 1979, while working a circular trip from London Bridge via Sutton back to London Bridge. The box was in use from 28th April 1929 until 16th April 1990. The siding on the left is the goods yard headshunt and in the background is the goods line to Raynes Park. After a long period of absence, a connection between the Central and South Western divisions in this vicinity was reinstated on 23rd September 1991. Two links facing opposite directions were provided. (J.N.Faulkner)

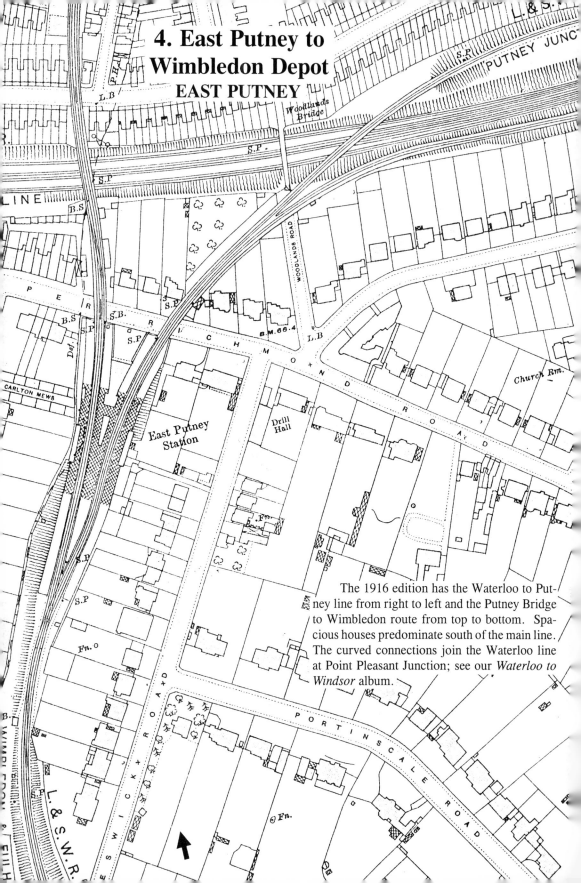

# 4. East Putney to Wimbledon Depot
## EAST PUTNEY

L. & S.

S.R. PUTNEY JUNC

Woodlands Bridge

WOODLANDS ROAD

LINE

CARLTON MEWS

East Putney Station

Drill Hall

Church Rm.

RICHMOND ROAD

BM.66.4

The 1916 edition has the Waterloo to Putney line from right to left and the Putney Bridge to Wimbledon route from top to bottom. Spacious houses predominate south of the main line. The curved connections join the Waterloo line at Point Pleasant Junction; see our *Waterloo to Windsor* album.

Fn.

KESWICK ROAD

PORTINSCALE ROAD

L. & S.W.R.

72. A rural ambience was created by the climb-
ing plants which covered the embankment walls
that flanked the entrance. The population grew
from 9400 in 1871 to over 24000 thirty years
later. (D.Cullum coll.)

73. A locomotive on a Metropolitan District
train displays its exhaust steam condensing pipes
which were so necessary on the underground
part of its journey. It is waiting to depart for
Wimbledon. (Lens of Sutton)

74. Unit no. S4412 stands at the up Waterloo platform with stencil in place ready to depart for Wimbledon. The circumstances of this unusual activity were not recorded. It was either working "wrong line" or had terminated here. The gradient is 1 in 58 down to Point Pleasant Junction and 1 in 60 up from it.
(Lens of Sutton)

75. The last down train from Waterloo to call for passengers was in July 1941 and so the shelter was subsequently demolished, leaving only a barrier round the steps. The reverse curves are of 16, 17 and 12 chains radius.
(Lens of Sutton)

76. A 1965 view shows Putney in transition with the erection of more office blocks. Note that the District Line centre conductor rail is on wooden blocks. Both types of return current system were in use between here and Wimble-don and bridging resistances were installed at the boundary with LT. There was a nominal difference of 50 volts between the two systems. (J.N.Faulkner)

77. Class Q1 0-6-0 no. 33027 approaches East Putney box with empty milk tankers from Morden South on 12th August 1965, bound for Clapham Junction. There is a trailing crossover in front of the box, which was built in 1889 and had 24 levers. (R.E.Ruffell)

78. Empty stock from Waterloo runs slowly over the curves on 3rd September 1990. The corresponding up line had been taken out of use on 4th April 1987 owing to deterioration of the viaduct. The remaining line was resignalled for reversible working on 16th September 1990, when Point Pleasant box closed. East Putney box closed on 25th February 1991. (V.Mitchell)

79. Another 1990 view shows the small shelter that replaced the extensive canopy over platforms 2 and 3. Weeds cover platform 4 and the track at platform 3. The steps to the former have been roofed, presumably to prevent rain from flooding the subway. (V.Mitchell)

80. No. 34109 *Sir Trafford Leigh-Mallory* eases the Clapham Junction to Templecombe milk empties round the 12-chain curve under the footbridge between Keswick Road and Lytton Grove on 4th July 1959. If the train was of more than 24 wagons, it was supposed to be double headed to Wimbledon.(S.C.Nash)

81. The LCGB railtour on 5th March 1967 runs north behind no. 34087 *145 Squadron* and is about to enter the 311yd long East Putney Tunnel under West Hill. On the left is Cromer Road Box which was in use until 29th November 1970, when colour light signals were introduced on the route.(J.Scrace)

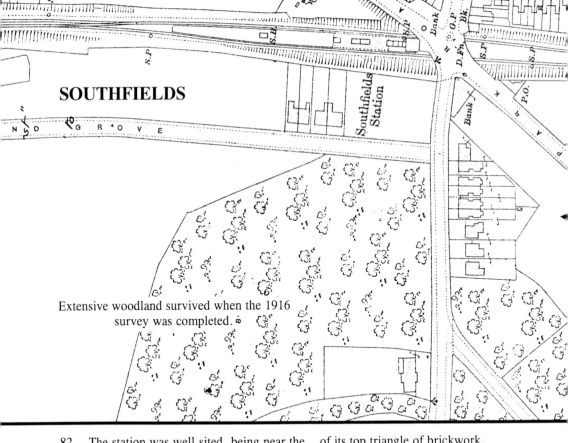

SOUTHFIELDS

Extensive woodland survived when the 1916
survey was completed.

82.   The station was well sited, being near the
junction of six roads. The dummy Dutch-style
gable was still present in 1996, although devoid
of its top triangle of brickwork.
(Lens of Sutton)

83.    The platform lines are on a gradient of 1 in 300 down to the bridge, beyond which the track rises at 1 in 241. The station was refurbished in 1991 at a cost of £103,000 and anti-vandal TV cameras were installed. (Lens of Sutton)

84.    The stationmasters house was set in a wooded triangle of land east of the station. Resident staff reduced the risk of vandalism. The house was an unusual subject for a postcard. (G.Gundry coll.)

85. A 1970 photograph features the down starting signal repeater, which was of value to guards. Also included is the footbridge which gave access to a side exit which was used to speed the departure of crowds visiting the nearby All England Tennis Championship Ground. (J.Scrace)

86. The box controlled a crossover north of the platform until 1946. To the south was Revelstoke Road box; both boxes closed on 29th November 1970, when colour lights were introduced. (Lens of Sutton)

87. A 1977 southward view shows an "East-bound" District Line train approaching. Such services were subject to OPO (One Person Operation) from 4th November 1985. (British Rail)

88. Two 2HAP units (nos 4313 and 4201) approach the station from the north while working empty from Waterloo to Wimbledon Park sidings after the morning rush hour on 15th March 1989.(J.N.Faulkner)

**Use of emergency coupling arrangement.**—Sets of emergency buffing gear have been provided at Wimbledon, Wimbledon Park, Southfields, and East Putney stations, by the use of which a Southern or Metropolitan District Railway electric train can be propelled or hauled, as required, for the purpose of removing it from a section on the Wimbledon and East Putney line in case of breakdown. The buffing gear must in all cases be fixed on the draw gear of the Southern Railway train or engine.

Two types of buffing gear have been provided, one for use on a steam locomotive when that means is adopted for clearing a disabled Metropolitan District train from a section, and the other for use on electric trains only, i.e., to admit of a disabled electric train being cleared by another electric train, and care must be taken to see that the proper appliance is used according to circumstances. The sets are lettered in white " engine buffing gear " or " carriage buffing gear " to indicate their respective uses.

Before the defective train is moved, it is necessary to see that the coupling chain provided with each set of gear is first put on the draw-bar hook of the engine or Southern Railway electric train, then the emergency buffer placed in position, and the hook and link coupled to the side chains of the Metropolitan District train.

The buffing gear cannot be used for propelling purposes on that type of the Metropolitan District wide coaching stock fitted with buffer plates, which type of stock can be propelled by an engine or electric train without the buffing gear, but the coupling chain must be used in such circumstances and also for hauling such stock, when required.

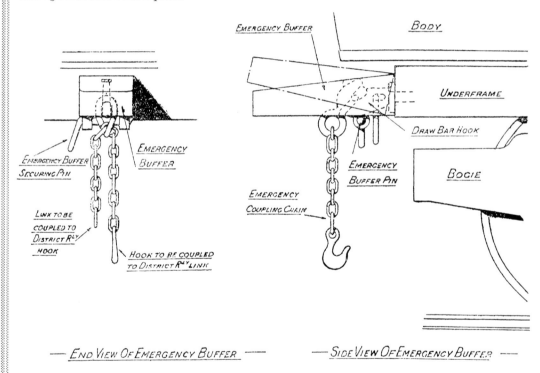

— *End View Of Emergency Buffer* —     — *Side View Of Emergency Buffer* —

INSTRUCTIONS FOR USE.

1. Emergency chain to be placed on drawbar hook
2. Emergency buffer lowered into position on drawbar hook
3. & Securely fastened by means of securing pin
4. Emergency chain coupled to side chains.

# WIMBLEDON PARK

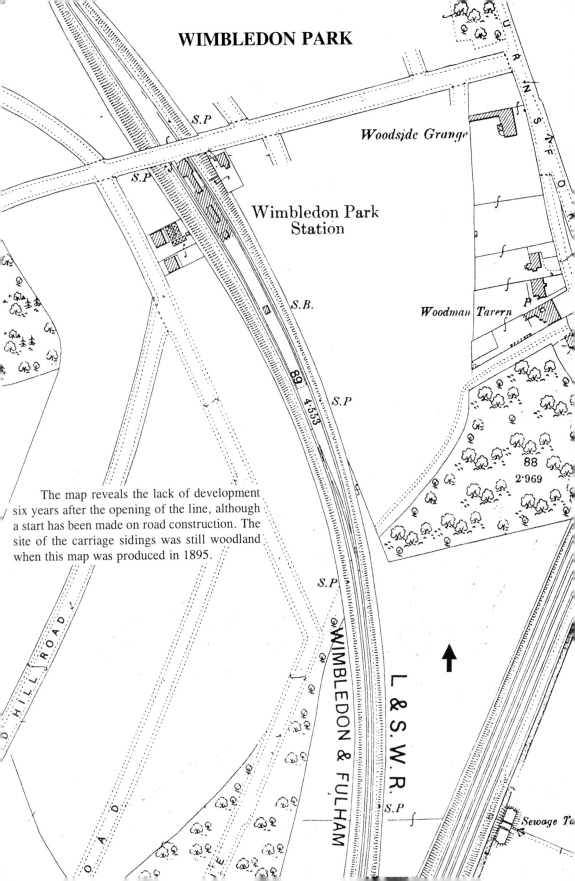

S.P

Woodside Grange

S.P

Wimbledon Park
Station

Woodman Tavern

S.B.

89.
4·553

S.P

88
2·969

The map reveals the lack of development
six years after the opening of the line, although
a start has been made on road construction. The
site of the carriage sidings was still woodland
when this map was produced in 1895.

S.P

S.P

HILL ROAD

WIMBLEDON & FULHAM

L & S.W.R.

S.P

Sewage T

89. Wimbledon Park with its fine lake was a great attraction to potential residents and soon elegant villas lined the surrounding roads and season ticket business traffic expanded accordingly. Even the cutting was wooded. (Lens of Sutton)

90. The gradient falls at 1 in 277 from the north and climbs at 1 in 260 from the bridge with the inevitable result if drains are not adequate. Note the masks on the signals to prevent the setting sun giving a false indication. (Lens of Sutton)

91.  The Southern Counties Touring Society's "Thamesider Special" railtour called on 31st May 1959, propelled by class M7 0-4-4T no.30050. Railway accountants in that era considered that a profit was made after fuel and crew had been paid, as stock and track already existed. Everyone benefitted accordingly. (A.E.Bennett)

92.  The box was photographed on 4th February 1970 and closed on 24th February 1991. In addition to being a block post, it controlled access to the carriage sidings from the East Putney line. (J.Scrace)

93.   A train of District Line Metadyne stock departs for Edgware Road as local passengers from Wimbledon leave the station on 28th May 1973. Southern Region trains at this time were either empty or specials.  (F.Hornby)

94.   The modest but stylish exterior was photographed on the same day. There was no indication of the train operator or of possible destinations, the disadvantage of the former not owning the station.(F.Hornby)

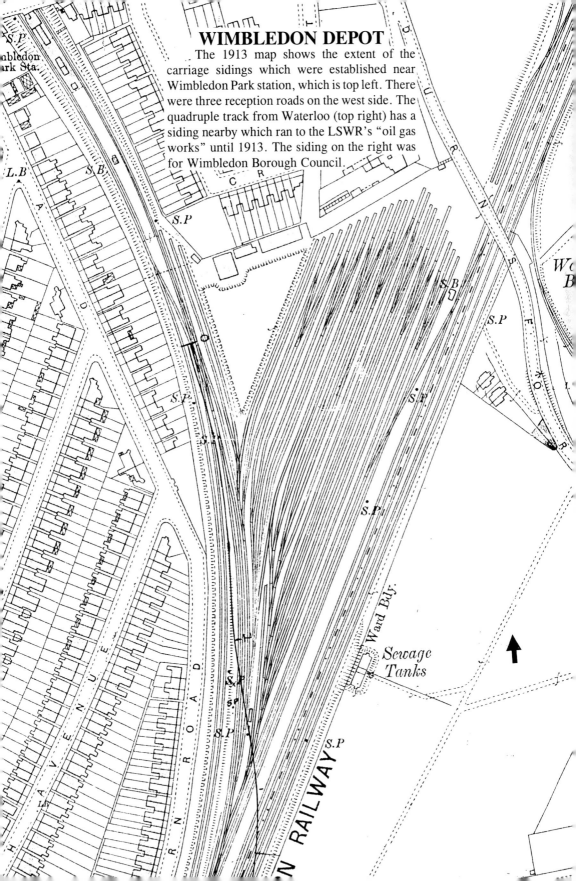

# WIMBLEDON DEPOT

The 1913 map shows the extent of the carriage sidings which were established near Wimbledon Park station, which is top left. There were three reception roads on the west side. The quadruple track from Waterloo (top right) has a siding nearby which ran to the LSWR's "oil gas works" until 1913. The siding on the right was for Wimbledon Borough Council.

95.    A photograph from 25th February 1922 has the WBC refuse destructor and electricity works  in the background and the East Putney lines in the foreground. No. 50 was one of the 0415 class built by Stephenson in 1883 and was scrapped in 1927. (H.C.Casserley)

96.    The Waterloo to Wimbledon line is from top to bottom and the platform of Wimbledon Park station is lower left. Durnsford Road Power station is top centre. It generated AC at 11kv for distribution over the entire LSWR electrified system. Reduction to 600 volts DC took place at a number of trackside substations housing rotary convertors. (Lens of Sutton)

97.   The building housed sixteen boilers, their coal being fed by gravity from the high level siding instead of the more usual conveyors. Coal fell from the wagons into a bunker of 1400 ton capacity and thence onto chain grate stokers. Four additional boilers were provided later to supply the five turbo-alternators. The wooden cooling towers are in the background. The steel chimney on the right replaced the brick one destroyed by enemy action on 14th October 1940. (N.L.Browne)

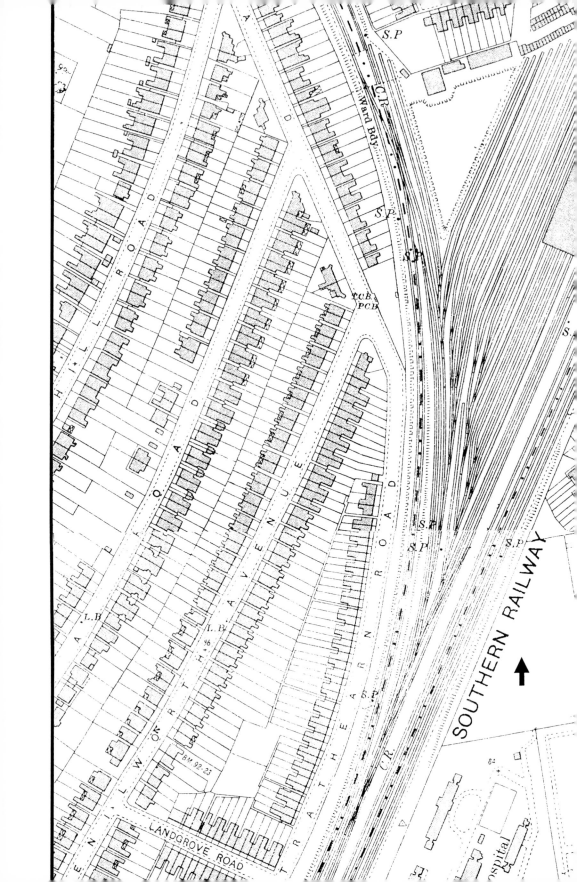

S.P

C.R.

Ward Bdy.

S.P.

S.P.

T.C.B.
P.C.B

S.P.

S.P.

S.P.

S.P.

S.P.

S.P.

C.R.

ROAD

ROAD

AVENUE

STRATHEARN ROAD

L.B.

L.B.

86

BM 92.23

LANDGROVE ROAD

SOUTHERN RAILWAY

Hospital

84

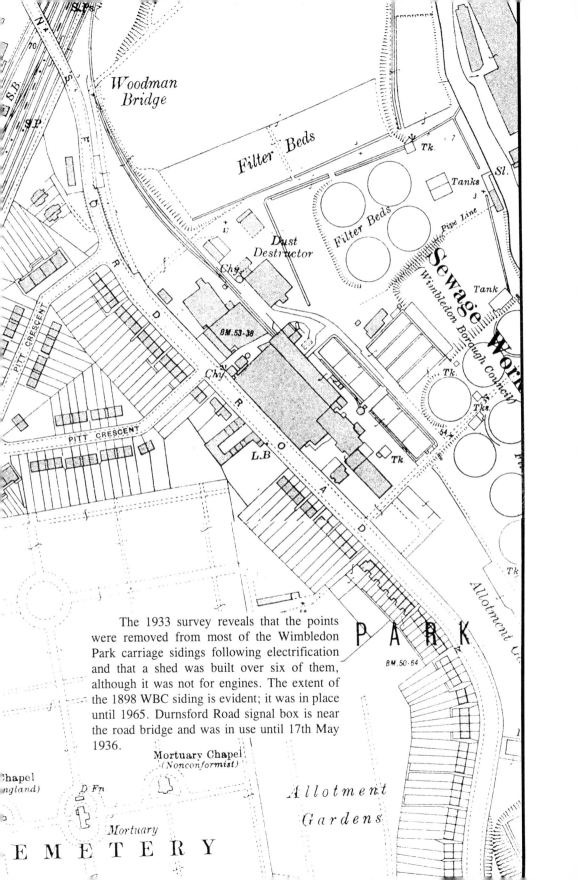

*Woodman Bridge*

*Filter Beds*

*Filter Beds*

Tk.

Tanks

Sl.

*Dust Destructor*

Pipe Line

Chy.

*Sewage Works*

*(Wimbledon Borough Council)*

Tank

BM.53·38

PITT CRESCENT

Chy.

Tk.

PITT CRESCENT

Tks.

L.B

Tk.

PARK

BM.50·64

The 1933 survey reveals that the points were removed from most of the Wimbledon Park carriage sidings following electrification and that a shed was built over six of them, although it was not for engines. The extent of the 1898 WBC siding is evident; it was in place until 1965. Durnsford Road signal box is near the road bridge and was in use until 17th May 1936.

Allotment

Tk.

Chapel ngland)

D Fn

Mortuary Chapel *(Nonconformist)*

*Allotment*

*Gardens*

*Mortuary*

E M E T E R Y

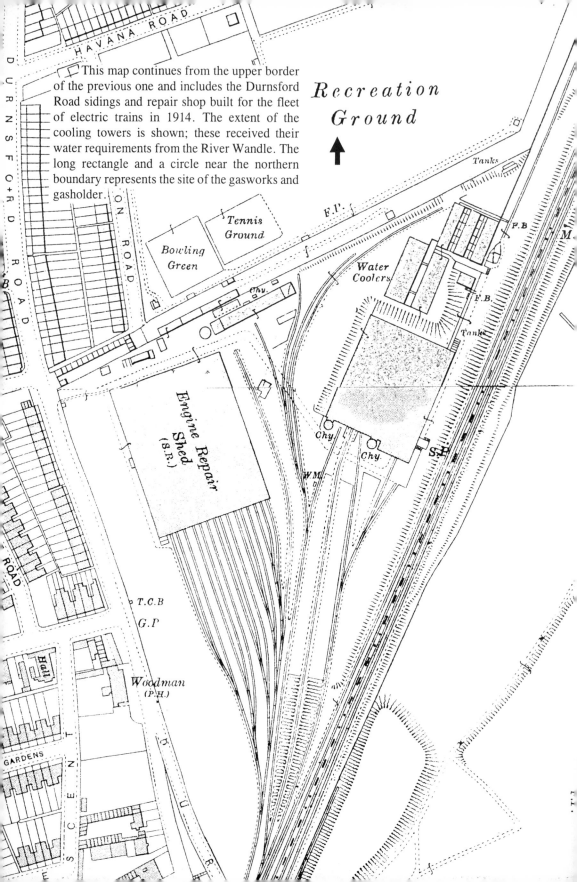

HAVANA ROAD

DURNSFORD ROAD

ON ROAD

*Recreation Ground*

This map continues from the upper border of the previous one and includes the Durnsford Road sidings and repair shop built for the fleet of electric trains in 1914. The extent of the cooling towers is shown; these received their water requirements from the River Wandle. The long rectangle and a circle near the northern boundary represents the site of the gasworks and gasholder.

*Tennis Ground*

*Bowling Green*

*F.P.*

Tanks

P.B.

M.

*Water Coolers*

F.B.

Tanks

Chy.

*Engine Repair Shed (S.R.)*

Chy.

Chy.

S.B.

W.M.

TYNCENT ROAD

T.C.B

G.P

*Woodman (P.H.)*

GARDENS

V I N C E N T

98. A concrete viaduct carried the siding to the top of the boiler house and this unique Bo-Bo electric locomotive pushed the coal wagons up the incline. Numbered by the SR 74S, it had been built to haul coal to the Waterloo & City Railway power station from the bottom of the Armstrong lift shaft. That station closed at about the time that this one opened. The locomotive is now the property of the National Railway Museum. (Unknown)

99. The bridge for Durnsford Road and the power station chimneys are in the background as the line leading to the WBC siding is upgraded and fitted with a conductor rail so that it could be used temporarily as the down local line during construction of the flyover in 1935-36. (R.Shepherd)

100.   A District Line train approaches the end of its journey with its return destination showing on 2nd March 1957. The flyover is beyond the carriage washing plant. The connection between the East Putney route and the main lines was reduced to a single line in 1989.  (R.C.Riley)

# SOUTHERN RAILWAY

## CHEAP "MONTHLY RETURN" TICKETS

# From Wimbledon, Malden and Epsom

CIRCULAR TOUR TICKETS AT REDUCED FARES FOR BUSINESS OR PLEASURE. APPLY BOOKING OFFICE.

### ANY DAY—ANY TRAIN—ANYWHERE
(except "Liner" and "Continental Boat" Trains)

Forward or Return—ANY DAY WITHIN ONE MONTH
(For one round trip)

WITH BREAK OF JOURNEY AT ANY INTERMEDIATE STATION.

Minimum Fares :—1st class **7 / 6**, 3rd class **5 / -.**

| TO | RETURN FARES, 3rd Class, FROM | | | TO | RETURN FARES, 3rd Class, FROM | | |
|---|---|---|---|---|---|---|---|
| | Wimbledon | Malden | Epsom | | Wimbledon | Malden | Epsom |
| | s. d. | s. d. | s. d. | | s. d. | s. d. | s. d. |
| ABERDEEN | 88 / 3 | 88 / 6 | 89 / 3 | LINCOLN | 24 / 2 | 24 / 8 | 25 / 2 |
| ARUNDEL | 8 / 8 | 8 / 8 | 7 / 7 | LITTLEHAMPTON | 9 / 5 | 9 / 2 | 8 / 2 |
| ASHFORD (Kent) (A) | 11 / - | 11 / 7 | 12 / 4 | LIVERPOOL | 36 / - | 36 / 3 | 37 / - |
| AXMINSTER | 25 / 6 | 25 / 6 | 27 / 10 | LLANDUDNO | 41 / 3 | 41 / 6 | 42 / - |
| AYR | 70 / 1 | 70 / 4 | 71 / 1 | LYME REGIS | 26 / 9 | 26 / 9 | 28 / 11 |
| BARNSTAPLE | 33 / 1 | 33 / 1 | 35 / 2 | LYMINGTON TOWN | 17 / 1 | 17 / 1 | — |
| BASINGSTOKE | 8 / 5 | 8 / 5 | 10 / 9 | MAIDSTONE | 8 / 5 | 8 / 11 | 9 / 5 |
| BEMBRIDGE (C) | 16 / 6 | 16 / 6 | 14 / 8 | MANCHESTER | 33 / 7 | 33 / 10 | 34 / 8 |
| BEXHILL (A) | 11 / 10 | 12 / 4 | 13 / 2 | MARGATE (A) | 13 / 8 | 14 / 2 | 15 / - |
| BIDEFORD | 34 / 8 | 34 / 8 | 36 / 9 | NEWCASTLE-ON-TYNE | 49 / 1 | 49 / 4 | 49 / 11 |
| BIRMINGHAM | 20 / 9 | 21 / - | 22 / 1 | NEWHAVEN TOWN (B) | 10 / 3 | 10 / 6 | — |
| BLACKPOOL | 41 / 3 | 41 / 6 | 42 / - | NEWPORT, I.W. (C) | 17 / 1 | 17 / 1 | 15 / 3 |
| BOGNOR REGIS | 10 / 3 | 10 / 3 | 9 / 2 | NORWICH | 21 / 6 | 22 / 1 | 22 / 7 |
| BOSCOMBE | 18 / 11 | 18 / 11 | 21 / - | OBAN | 89 / 3 | 89 / 6 | 90 / 3 |
| BOURNEMOUTH CTL. | 18 / 11 | 18 / 11 | 21 / 3 | OKEHAMPTON | 34 / 8 | 34 / 8 | 36 / 9 |
| BRIGHTON | 9 / 2 | 9 / 9 | 8 / 2 | PADSTOW | 44 / 11 | 44 / 11 | 47 / 3 |
| BRISTOL | 22 / 1 | 22 / 7 | 23 / 1 | PLYMOUTH | 39 / 8 | 39 / 8 | 41 / 9 |
| BROADSTAIRS | 14 / 5 | 14 / 8 | 15 / 6 | POOLE | 19 / 11 | 19 / 11 | 22 / 4 |
| BROCKENHURST | 16 / 3 | 16 / 3 | — | PORTLAND | 25 / 9 | 25 / 9 | 28 / 1 |
| BUDE | 40 / 2 | 40 / 2 | 42 / 3 | PORTSLADE | 9 / 5 | 10 / - | 7 / 11 |
| CANTERBURY EAST | 12 / 1 | 12 / 7 | 13 / 2 | PORTSMOUTH & S'SEA | 13 / 2 | 13 / 2 | 11 / 3 |
| CARDIFF | 28 / 1 | 28 / 7 | 29 / 2 | RAMSGATE (A) | 14 / 8 | 15 / 3 | 15 / 9 |
| CARLISLE | 53 / 10 | 54 / 1 | 54 / 10 | READING | 7 / 4E | 6 / 10E | 7 / 7F |
| CHATHAM (A) | 6 / 10 | 7 / 4 | 8 / 2 | ROCHESTER (A) | 6 / 10 | 7 / 4 | 8 / 2 |
| CHICHESTER | 10 / 9 | 10 / 9 | 9 / 5 | RYDE ESPLANADE (C) | 15 / 3 | 15 / 3 | 13 / 8 |
| CHRISTCHURCH | 18 / 5 | 18 / 5 | 20 / 6 | ST. LEONARDS (A) | 11 / 10 | 12 / 4 | 13 / 2 |
| COWES (C) | 17 / 10 | 17 / 10 | 16 / - | SALISBURY | 14 / 8 | 14 / 8 | 17 / 1A |
| DEAL | 15 / 9 | 16 / - | 16 / 10 | SANDOWN (C) | 15 / 6 | 16 / 6 | 14 / 8 |
| DEVONPORT | 39 / 8 | 39 / 8 | 41 / 9 | SANDWICH | 15 / 9 | 16 / - | — |
| DORCHESTER | 23 / 11 | 23 / 11 | 26 / 3 | SCARBOROUGH | 41 / 9 | 42 / - | 42 / 9 |
| DOVER | 14 / 8 | 15 / - | 15 / - | SEAFORD (B) | 10 / 6 | 11 / - | — |
| DUNDEE | 80 / 7 | 80 / 10 | 81 / 7 | SEATON | 27 / - | 27 / - | 29 / 2 |
| EASTBOURNE | 11 / 7B | 11 / 10B | 13 / 5A | SHANKLIN (C) | 16 / 10 | 16 / 10 | 15 / - |
| EDINBURGH | 70 / 8 | 70 / 11 | 71 / 8 | SHEERNESS-ON-SEA | 8 / 11 | 9 / 5 | 10 / - |
| EXETER | 30 / 2 | 30 / 2 | 32 / 7 | SHEFFIELD | 29 / 2 | 29 / 8 | 30 / 2 |
| EXMOUTH | 31 / - | 31 / - | 33 / 1 | SIDMOUTH | 29 / 5 | 29 / 5 | 31 / 9 |
| FOLKESTONE | 13 / 5 | 13 / 11 | 14 / 8 | SOUTHAMPTON | 13 / 11 | 13 / 11 | 16 / - |
| FRATTON | 12 / 10 | 12 / 10 | 11 / 3 | SWANAGE | 23 / 1 | 23 / 1 | 25 / 6 |
| FRESHWATER (C) | 18 / 11 | 18 / 11 | 17 / 4 | TAVISTOCK | 37 / 6 | 37 / 6 | 39 / 11 |
| GILLINGHAM (Kent) (A) | 7 / 1 | 7 / 4 | 8 / 2 | VENTNOR (C) | 17 / 7 | 17 / 7 | 15 / 9 |
| GLASGOW | 71 / 8 | 71 / 11 | 72 / 9 | WADEBRIDGE | 44 / 8 | 44 / 8 | 47 / - |
| GLASTONBURY (D) | 22 / 4 | 22 / 4 | — | WALMER (A) | 15 / 3 | 15 / 9 | 16 / 6 |
| HASTINGS (A) | 12 / 1 | 12 / 7 | 13 / 2 | WESTGATE-ON-SEA | 13 / 5 | 13 / 11 | 14 / 8 |
| HAYLING ISLAND | 12 / 7 | 12 / 7 | 10 / 9 | WEYMOUTH | 25 / 2 | 25 / 2 | 27 / 4 |
| HERNE BAY | 12 / 4 | 12 / 7 | 13 / 5 | WHITSTABLE & TANK'N | 11 / 7 | 12 / 1 | 12 / 10 |
| HOVE | 9 / 2 | 9 / 9 | 7 / 11 | WINCHESTER | 11 / 7 | 11 / 7 | 13 / 11 |
| ILFRACOMBE | 35 / 5 | 35 / 5 | 37 / 10 | WORTHING CENTRAL | 10 / 9 | 11 / 3 | 8 / 5 |
| INVERNESS | 93 / 6 | 93 / 9 | 94 / 6 | YARMOUTH, I.W. (C) | 18 / 8 | 18 / 8 | 17 / 1 |
| LEEDS | 33 / 10 | 34 / 2 | 34 / 11 | YARMOUTH (GREAT) | 22 / 10 | 23 / 4 | 23 / 11 |
| LEICESTER | 18 / 5 | 18 / 11 | 19 / 5 | YEOVIL | 22 / 1 | 22 / 1 | 24 / 2 |
| LEWES | 9 / 2B | 9 / 5B | 11 / -A | YORK | 34 / 5 | 34 / 8 | 35 / 5 |

**CHILDREN UNDER 14, HALF-FARE.**     **FIRST CLASS TICKETS ALSO ISSUED.**

➤ FOR FARES TO OTHER PLACES, APPLY AT BOOKING OFFICE ◄

A—Via London.    B—Via Clapham Junction.    C—Via Portsmouth Harbour.    D—Via Templecombe.
E—Via Kingston.    F—Via Guildford.

Waterloo Station, S.E.1,
January, 1939.

GILBERT S. SZLUMPER,
General Manager.

Printed in Great Britain.
* Waterlow & Sons Limited, London and Dunstable.

101. A northward view from Durnsford Road bridge features the flyover which has carried the up local line over both main lines since 17th May 1936. Two 4SUB units are bound for Shepperton on 2nd March 1957 and run past the long berthing siding, which was shortened in 1984 and subsequently taken out of use. (R.C.Riley)

102. A northward view on 2nd September 1966 from almost the same viewpoint as picture no. 97 reveals that most of the power station had vanished, the National Grid providing power wherever it was required. Class 5 4-6-0 no. 73016 is working the 17.23 Waterloo to Bournemouth Central while two 4 COR units stand in the depot. (J.Scrace)

———————————►

103. The connections between the depot and the East Putney lines at Wimbledon Park can be seen in this photograph from 11th April 1970. Also featured are de-icing units nos. 015 and 019. (R.E.Ruffell)

———————————►

104. No. 019 is seen again, this time outside the 1914 repair shops on 18th October 1973. The sheds were demolished shortly afterwards to make way for the new East Wimbledon Depot, shown in pictures 107 and 108. (J.Scrace)

105.    A collision took place adjacent to the flyover on 21st July 1975. Being on sidings, no official report was published but rumours suggested that a controller had been tied down mischievously. Between the rear coach and the flyover is Top Yard Shunters box.
(British Rail)

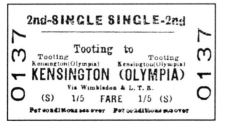

06.    This and the next three pictures were ken on 6th May 1991 during the depot open eekend. This includes the end of the flyover, e rear of a westbound fast train, the staff halt the up main line, the connection from the depot to this line and no.34027 *Taw Valley* on a shuttle service within the depot. Beyond the platform is Durnsford Road Shunters box. (V.Mitchell)

07.    The panorama from the other side of urnsford Road bridge includes the same train the distance, no. 50018 with a train for xeter, the depot's breakdown crane in action d a class 59 diesel on show outside the inspec-tion shed, which came into use on 22nd 1976. Roads 12 and 13 have heavy lifting facilities. Pits are available for 56 coaches to be examined simultaneously.  (V.Mitchell)

108. On the left is the shuttle train loading passengers and Earlsfield Shunters box, which is staffed almost continuously. To the right of the varied display of traction is the building that houses a wheel lathe that can reprofile a wheelset without it leaving the train. The dull weather was followed by a wet Sunday. (V.Mitchell)

109. Turning round, we see the 1976 connection to the up main line and Earlsfield station in the distance. To the left of the lighting masts is a shunting neck, which ends on the bank of the River Wandle. In 1990, the stores supplied 15800 new seat covers for class 455 units, 65000 brake blocks or pads and 10000 fluorescent tubes. (V.Mitchell)

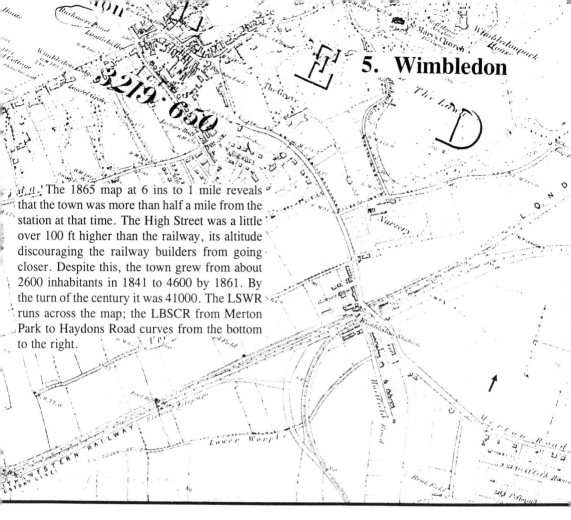

## 5. Wimbledon

The 1865 map at 6 ins to 1 mile reveals that the town was more than half a mile from the station at that time. The High Street was a little over 100 ft higher than the railway, its altitude discouraging the railway builders from going closer. Despite this, the town grew from about 2600 inhabitants in 1841 to 4600 by 1861. By the turn of the century it was 41000. The LSWR runs across the map; the LBSCR from Merton Park to Haydons Road curves from the bottom to the right.

110. The two companies had separate stations, although one island platform was common. The first LSWR station, however, was west of the road bridge until the 1880s. This is the company's second station, the terminus for trains from the Putney route being at the end of the station approach. On the left is the road to the goods yard. (Lens of Sutton)

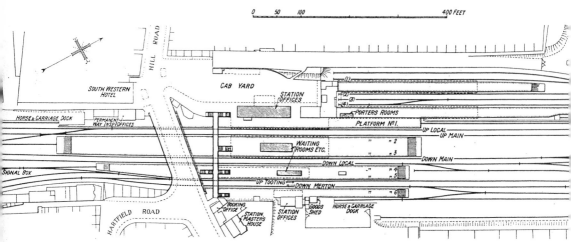

Plan before reconstruction.
(Railway Engineer)

111. The southern end of the footbridge shown in the previous picture is seen here spanning the ex-LBSCR platforms on 10th April 1926, as class T1 0-4-4T no. 363 waits to leave for Tulse Hill. Reference to the diagram will reveal that this platform was then numbered 5.
(H.C.Casserley)

112. The station was completely rebuilt in 1927-28. This transitional view is from platform 1 and shows the future platform 7(down through) taking shape in the background. Quad-ruple track had been provided to Malden in 1869 for the new Kingston service but both local lines were on the south side of the main tracks until 1884. (Lens of Sutton)

Plan after reconstruction.
(Railway Engineer)

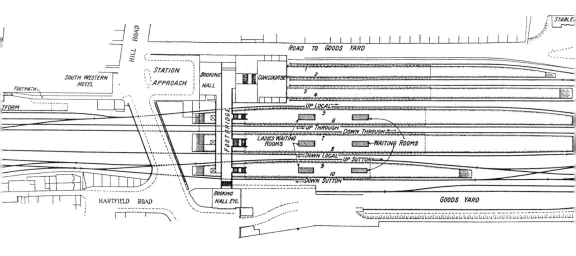

113. The road-level entrance is seen as the new all-concrete footbridge nears completion and modern station buildings arise in the back- ground. The LBSCR once had their own offices at the end of an approach road on the south side - see diagram. (Lens of Sutton)

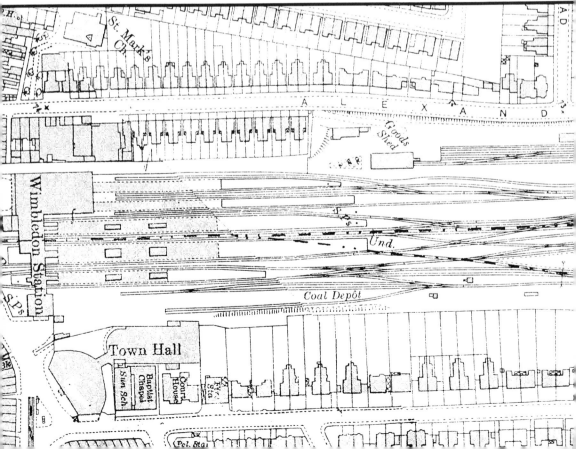

114.    Approaching platform 1 on 29th June 1935 is a District Line train of G stock carrying a *NON-STOP* board which indicated that certain stations were passed by. The line to Haydons Road passes under the bridge on the right, which carries Ashcombe Road. Alterations in this vicinity took place in 1913 in readiness for District Line trains to run to a proposed new line to Sutton but the advent of World War I altered this chapter of history.  (H.F.Wheeller)

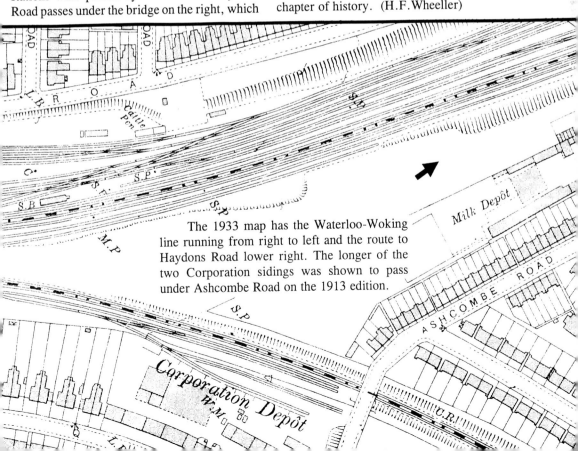

The 1933 map has the Waterloo-Woking line running from right to left and the route to Haydons Road lower right. The longer of the two Corporation sidings was shown to pass under Ashcombe Road on the 1913 edition.

115. Only the well informed would know that the train of K stock at platform 4 was destined for *Kensington* High Street. Also included in this photograph from 13th July 1954 is an ex-travelling post office vehicle, then serving as a temporary office. (J.H.Aston)

116. The points at the London end of the station were renewed on 28th November 1965, this necessitating some unusual working. The track from platform 5 had been slewed into bay platform 4 and a limited service of up trains to Waterloo was being diverted via East Putney. Here an up Kingston train is departing from no.5 under the authority of no. 4's semaphore signal. The roof of the goods shed is visible. (J.N.Faulkner)

SOUTHERN RAILWAY.
Available on the DATE of issue ONLY.
This ticket is issued subject to the Regulations
& Conditions stated in the Company's Time
Tables & Bills
O 982
MERTON ABBEY
TO
WIMBLEDON wi
THIRD CLASS.
2½d.     Fare     2½d.
O 982

117. The "Farewell to Steam" railtour on 20th September 1964 was appropriately hauled by the last locomotive built by BR, class 9F 2-10-0 no. 92220 *Evening Star*. It has just passed through Haydons Road and is entering platform 8. The connection was not used by regular passenger services then, although it had once carried flying boat passengers from Victoria to Southampton Docks. It was lifted in 1982. (J.Scrace)

118. At 19.48 on 12th October 1972, the 18.45 Acton to Wimbledon West Yard freight, hauled by electro-diesel class 73 no. E6001, ran into the stationary 19.05 from Holborn Viaduct. The driver had passed a red signal and also failed to apply the brakes. Although he smelt of alcohol, the law at that time did not require or allow blood or urine samples to be tested. (J.Scrace)

**Companion albums to feature this station -**
*Waterloo to Woking* (1986),
*Mitcham Junction Lines* (1992),
*Wimbledon to Epsom* (1995), **and**
*Kingston and Wimbledon Tramways* (1995)

119. An extremely novel train passed through platform 5 on 22nd July 1976. London Transport battery-electric locomotive no. 45 hauled ex-Metropolitan Railway brake third coach no. 519 to Ruislip Depot for refurbishing. It had been in store at Preston Park. (R.E.Ruffell)

120. Class 455 unit no. 5708 passes "A" Box on 2nd April 1995, while working the 14.17 Waterloo to Strawberry Hill service. The box was opened on 22nd February 1948 and ceased to control the main and local lines on 12th April 1990, remaining open until 25th February 1991 for the East Putney line only. District line trains run along the side of the site of the former LSWR goods yard, which closed to traffic on 5th January 1970. Wimbledon has become an important traffic centre and has an excellent train service, with more direct destinations than ever since the introduction of Thameslink services. (M.J.Stretton)

# MP Middleton Press

Easebourne Lane, Midhurst. West Sussex. GU29 9AZ    Tel: 01730 813169  Fax: 01730 812601

*. . . . . Write or telephone for our latest list . . . . .*

## BRANCH LINES
Branch Line to Allhallows
Branch Lines to Alton
Branch Lines around Ascot
Branch Line to Bude
Branch Lines around Canterbury
Branch Lines to East Grinstead
Branch Lines around Effingham Jn
Branch Lines to Exmouth
Branch Line to Fairford
Branch Line to Hawkhurst
Branch Lines to Horsham
Branch Lines around Huntingdon
Branch Lines to Ilfracombe
Branch Line to Lyme Regis
Branch Line to Lynton
Branch Lines around March
Branch Lines around Midhurst
Branch Lines to Newport
Branch Line to Padstow
Branch Lines around Portmadoc 1923-46
Branch Lines around Porthmadog 1954-94
Branch Lines to Seaton & Sidmouth
Branch Line to Selsey
Branch Lines around Sheerness
Branch Line to Southwold
Branch Line to Swanage
Branch Line to Tenterden
Branch Lines to Torrington
Branch Lines to Tunbridge Wells
Branch Line to Upwell
Branch Lines around Weymouth

## LONDON SUBURBAN RAILWAYS
Caterham and Tattenham Corner
Clapham Jn. to Beckenham Jn.
Crystal Palace and Catford Loop
Holborn Viaduct to Lewisham
London Bridge to Addiscombe
Mitcham Junction Lines
South London Line
West Croydon to Epsom
Willesden Junction to Richmond
Wimbledon to Epsom

## STEAMING THROUGH
Steaming through Cornwall
Steaming through East Sussex
Steaming through the Isle of Wight
Steaming through Surrey
Steaming through West Hants
Steaming through West Sussex

## GREAT RAILWAY ERAS
Ashford from Steam to Eurostar
Festiniog in the Fifties

## COUNTRY BOOKS
Brickmaking in Sussex
East Grinstead Then and Now

## SOUTH COAST RAILWAYS
Ashford to Dover
Bournemouth to Weymouth
Brighton to Eastbourne
Brighton to Worthing
Chichester to Portsmouth
Dover to Ramsgate
Hastings to Ashford
Ryde to Ventnor
Worthing to Chichester

## SOUTHERN MAIN LINES
Bromley South to Rochester
Charing Cross to Orpington
Crawley to Littlehampton
Dartford to Sittingbourne
East Croydon to Three Bridges
Epsom to Horsham
Exeter to Barnstaple
Exeter to Tavistock
Faversham to Dover
Haywards Heath to Seaford
London Bridge to East Croydon
Orpington to Tonbridge
Sittingbourne to Ramsgate
Swanley to Ashford
Three Bridges to Brighton
Tonbridge to Hastings
Victoria to Bromley South
Waterloo to Windsor
Woking to Southampton
Yeovil to Exeter

## COUNTRY RAILWAY ROUTES
Andover to Southampton
Bath to Evercreech Junction
Bournemouth to Evercreech Jn
Burnham to Evercreech Junction
Croydon to East Grinstead
East Kent Light Railway
Fareham to Salisbury
Guildford to Redhill
Porthmadog to Blaenau
Reading to Basingstoke
Reading to Guildford
Redhill to Ashford
Salisbury to Westbury
Strood to Paddock Wood
Taunton to Barnstaple
Westbury to Bath
Woking to Alton

## TROLLEYBUS CLASSICS
Croydon's Trolleybuses
Woolwich & Dartford Trolleybuses

## TRAMWAY CLASSICS
Aldgate & Stepney Tramways
Bournemouth & Poole Tramways
Brighton's Tramways
Bristol's Tramways
Camberwell & W. Norwood Tramways
Croydon's Tramways
Dover's Tramways
East Ham & West Ham Tramways
Embankment & Waterloo Tramways
Exeter & Taunton Tramways
Greenwich & Dartford Tramways
Hampstead & Highgate Tramways
Hastings Tramways
Ilford & Barking Tramways
Kingston & Wimbledon Tramways
Lewisham & Catford Tramways
Maidstone & Chatham Tramways
North Kent Tramways
Portsmouth's Tramways
Southampton Tramways
Southend-on-sea Tramways
Thanet's Tramways
Victoria & Lambeth Tramways
Walthamstow & Leyton Tramways
Wandsworth & Battersea Tramways

## OTHER RAILWAY BOOKS
Garraway Father & Son
Industrial Railways of the South East
London Chatham & Dover Railway
South Eastern Railway
War on the Line

## MILITARY BOOKS
Battle over Portsmouth
Battle Over Sussex 1940
Blitz Over Sussex 1941-42
Bognor at War
Bombers over Sussex 1943-45
Military Defence of West Sussex

## WATERWAY ALBUMS
Hampshire Waterways
Kent and East Sussex Waterways
London to Portsmouth Waterway
West Sussex Waterways

## BUS BOOK
Eastbourne Bus Story

## SOUTHERN RAILWAY
## ● VIDEOS ●
Memories of the Hayling Island Branch
Memories of the Lyme Regis Branch
War on the Line